Have Books Will Travel

Your Guide to Selling Your Paperbacks
at Live Events

Judith A. Barrett

WC
Wobbly Creek

Wobbly Creek LLC

Have Books Will Travel: Your Guide to Selling Your Paperbacks at Live Events

Published in the United States of America by Wobbly Creek, LLC

2025 Georgia

wobblycreek.com

Cover by Wobbly Creek, LLC

ISBN 978-1-967288-22-9 eBook

ISBN 978-1-967288-23-6 Paperback

Contents

Welcome!

Hey there and welcome! I'm so glad you picked up this book.

Maybe you're just thinking about selling your books in person and want to know what it's really like. Or maybe you've already done a few events and are looking for ways to improve your setup, boost your sales, and enjoy the experience a little more.

Either way, you're in the right place.

Selling books in person is one of the most rewarding, and sometimes unexpected, parts of being an author. Sure, it can be tiring, and there's a lot to figure out at first. But those moments when your stories connect with readers face-to-face? They're unforgettable.

At one of my favorite events, a young girl came to my table, eyes wide, and said, "I've read this. And this. And this," as she pointed to all six books in a series. "My favorite author wrote these."

Then she stared at me. "And now YOU'RE HERE!" Cue the tears.

Her grandfather stood behind her and beamed at us while we discussed which series she should read next then he quietly paid for the three books she picked out to start a new series. My hand shook as I signed her books because I was so excited for her. And, honestly, for me. She reminded me why I do this.

I'm living proof you don't need a fancy booth or a background in sales to make an impact. You just need your books, a little planning, and a willingness to show up. That's what this guide is all about. I'm sharing practical tips, honest advice, and everything I've learned over the years from actual events with real readers.

So whether you're just starting or refining your setup, welcome to your next chapter. You've got stories to share and readers to meet, and I can't wait to help you get there.

Chapter 1: My Journey

WHO AM I?

Now that we're off to a good start (and maybe a little misty-eyed), you might be wondering *who is this person who's giving advice about hauling books to festivals and chatting up strangers next to a kettle corn stand?*

Fair question.

Over the past seven years, I've written and published over fifty books with more to come. At the same time, I've also been selling my books face-to-face at a variety of events. So before we get into the how-to, let me tell you a little about how I got here.

I began writing after a rich and varied career in the corporate world, and I draw from my background and life experiences to create characters who are brave, flawed, and unforgettable.

My genres are thriller, mystery, cozy mystery, historical fiction, and post-apocalyptic sci-fi. All of my books have a touch of paranormal. I'm not your typical author, and I don't write typical stories. I don't stay in one genre lane because my goal is to have a book for any reader who stops at my table at events.

My promise to my readers is *You keep reading; I'll keep writing!*

Vendor

I sell paperbacks in person at craft festivals, local book fairs, library and school events, and book cons around the Southeast, where I connect with readers face-to-face.

While each type of event has its own vibe and logistics, the core principles are the same: The one-on-one connection with readers matters to me, and I wouldn't do it if it wasn't fun!

I've built an online shop as an extension of meeting readers, expanded into author merch, and continue to grow because I believe in telling good stories, and in the power of readers to find them.

NOT YOUR TYPICAL VENDOR

Are you thinking I must be an outgoing, congenial, maybe even a slightly pushy salesperson?

I'm not. I'm claustrophobic in crowds, socially awkward, and horrible at small talk. My idea of a good time is staying home with my Hubs and dogs while I write a book. I love the idea of a party, but I'd rather clean out a closet than actually go to one.

So, how can I be so excited about trekking to events with my books? My stories are captivating, and I know it. I enjoy talking to people one-on-one, and I can talk about books and listen to people talk about what they like to read and why all day long. I learn something new from every reader at every event.

Tip: I've uncovered the best kept marketing research secret in the world. If you want to know what people like to read, set up a table with your books on it. When people slow down and pause at your table, you're in the presence of a reader. Ask them, "What do you like to read?"

Bonus: watch their eyes. They'll tell you which cover they like.

Vendor and Author

I've attended events that are held inside and outside. The set up might be different, but the basics are the same. Besides being a book creator aka author, I'm a vendor. My art is writing, and my craft is my book and publishing.

Tip: People who sell products at events are vendors who know how to display their products to catch a browser's eye and how to turn an interested browser into a happy buyer. I follow their examples and think like they do.

When you're a vendor at an arts and crafts or festival event, it isn't a gathering of authors; it's a festival with vendors, and one of them is an author: you, a vendor-author. You'll be alongside hand-carved signs, crocheted hats, local pottery, and kid face-painting squads. You'll see the tools, personality, and hustle of vendors at a festival. I've discovered there is so much to learn from the vendors you meet at fairs and festival events.

When you're an author-vendor at a book event with other author-vendors, you have a bond: you've been through the same struggles and heartaches to write, polish, and publish your books.

You'll be surrounded by authors with a variety of skills. You'll observe authors first-hand who excel at booth display, those who excel at pre-selling, and authors who draw even the most reluctant reader into an engaging discussion. And what a great opportunity to network with your peers!

When you show up to any event excited to learn, you'll be doing more than selling books; you'll be connecting with readers and vendors. Genuine connections make you a better vendor and bring readers back to the event the following year looking for you.

I love it when a reader rushes to my booth and pounds on the table. "I need my next book!"

Gives me the shivers every time! I suspect it will be the same for you.

Let's get this hustle going! But first...

Before your First Event

Like a painter with their canvas, your book is your product, a tangible representation of your creativity and effort.

'Don't judge a book by its cover' might be sage advice, but that's exactly what readers are doing when they approach your table. The title, imagery, and cover art set their expectation of what they'll find between the pages.

THE BACK OF YOUR BOOKS

While you and the reader are chatting about what they like to read and why, your reader picks up a book and turns it over, which is exactly what we want them to do.

The cover caught their eye; now they want to learn more.

A wise author once told me when a reader picks up your book, they're establishing a connection, almost an ownership, with the book. My thought is the longer they hold the book, the deeper the connection, and the more likely they are to want to take "their" book home.

What catches their eye on the backs of my books while they're reading the blurb and my bio?

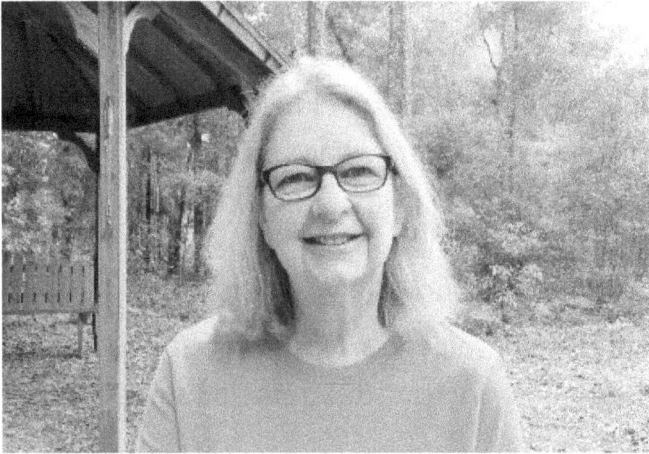

Judith A. Barrett, Author. My photo is on the back of all my paperbacks.

I've watched as readers read the blurb then examine my photo. The back of my books creates a powerful connection when readers realize, "Oh, you're the author!"

If you use a pen name or have another reason that you aren't using an author photo, consider other options for the readers to ponder while they look at the back of your book. What do you have that represents you? Your logo? If I didn't use my photo and was writing with a pen name, I'd have a sketch of a dog maybe with a cat because all my books have at least one dog in them, and I don't want to leave out the occasional cat that wanders into the stories.

Types of Events

All in-person events are either indoor or outdoor. While the basics for selling your books to readers are the same, we'll discuss the differences in setup as we go along.

The setups for different indoor events have unique requirements. We'll look at the unique adjustments for the different indoor events in Chapter Ten.

Chapter 2: Getting Started

While each type of direct sales event has its own vibe and logistics, the core principles are the same: make your booth inviting and listen more than talk to readers.

Getting started doesn't have to be overwhelming. Start small, be prepared, and treat every event as a learning opportunity. If you're willing to adjust when things don't go as expected, you'll be ahead of the game and more prepared for your next event.

MY FIRST EVENT

My first in-person event as a vendor was seven years ago at a Ham Radio Fest. The vendors outside of the building had their antennas, amateur radio gear and supplies displayed in the beds of their pickups or in the open trunks of their cars.

I was inside a small metal building that was the partially cleared storage building for an amateur radio club. I had six copies of my one published book, a children's book that was published by a small press. I was there because I had a great story and knew it.

I covered the ham radio club's table with a pink tablecloth and had a signup sheet for my newsletter and an 8.5" x 11" sign announcing the award my book had won. The event organizers positioned me near the front door, which was a prime spot.

At the ham fest, I sold one book for ten dollars. The ten dollar vendor fee was waived because I was a member. I made ten dollars selling a book, and I was hooked.

Finding the Right Events

Not all events are created equal, especially for selling books. You might think more foot traffic equals more sales, but that's not always the case. The best events are where your readers are at the event to buy. Your goal is to develop a discerning eye to recognize those gems.

Tip: If the event has photos of past years, look for how many vendors there are and how many visitors have stopped at booths or are milling about or strolling through the aisles or pathway. Just because there are visitors doesn't mean your sales will excel, but if there are very few visitors, that's a flag to ask for more information.

EVENTS TO CONSIDER

- Outdoor events in spring and fall.

- Indoor events in summer and winter.

- Arts and crafts festivals.

- Local festivals sponsored by civic groups or towns.

- Book conferences in your main genre.

- Book fairs sponsored local or state writer groups.

- Book fairs at nearby community colleges or libraries.

- Comic cons: Best for graphic novels, science fiction, fantasy, or horror. Bonus: cosplay.

Tip #1: Determine the number of hours you'd be on your feet. 10:00 AM-4:00 PM is great. 10:00 AM-10:00 PM is not.

Tip #2: Attend events as a visitor and talk to the vendors.

How to Find Events

- Local organizations: Kiwanis, Chamber of Commerce, or City-sponsored. These are my favorites.

- Facebook Groups for authors or crafters.

- Word-of-mouth from other vendors.

- Eventbrite and FestivalNet.com.

Tip: Some events are "cashless." All payments are handled by the event organizers through a bracelet or digital system. I'm leery of them.

Questions to Ask

- What was the attendance last year?

- What type of vendors are allowed? Specific genre only? Arts and crafts only?

Commercial? Third-party sales?

Tip #1: If the event sounds sketchy, has high fees, or vague promises ("Our first year and we expect 10,000 people!"), it might be a pass. Better to miss one than burn out early. Burnout by heartbreak is real.

Tip #2: If you skip an event because you have doubts, attend it as a visitor to scope it out for next year.

You Are a Vendor

Before you go to your first event, educate yourself about sales tax and your state. I report and pay my sales tax without fail.

Most states occasionally spot check events to be sure all the vendors are registered with the state. Just take care of it now.

Start with the Bare Necessities

You do *not* need to go all out your first time. Sometimes first-time authors have invested hundreds of dollars in event gear they never used again, or worse, after one event, they decide direct sell isn't for them after all.

Tip: Start small, talk to other vendors, and build up your gear list based on what works for you.

Your Essential Starter Kit

- Your books.

- Folding table(s). 4–6 feet collapsible, lightweight with a handle to carry. (unless event provides tables)

- Tablecloth. Any solid color works. White or black, or better yet, what's your brand color?

- *Outdoor event*: 10ft x 10ft canopy tent and weights.

- A price sign that includes your volume discount prices.

- Sign with <Your Name>, Author. Add your tagline and genre(s).

- Chair for you and a chair for your Event Buddy.

- Pen(s) for signing books.

- Notebook and pen to record sales.

- Water. More important than you think.

- Comfortable shoes.

- *Outdoor event*: Sunscreen and a hat.

Bare Minimum Rule

If your gear doesn't fit in the trunk of your car or in the bed of your truck, and you can't set up in less than 45 minutes, it's too much for your first event.

Add ons for Your Starter Kit

- Business cards.

- Cash box that locks.

- Mobile credit card reader.

- Fully charged cell phone.

- Lunch and snacks.

- *Outdoor Event*: Folding wagon or cart.

  - Holds at least 100 lbs.

  - Collapsible and fits in your vehicle.

- ○ Rugged wheels for dirt or gravel paths.

- *Outdoor Event*: Lighting for an evening event.

- *Indoor Event*: Folding hand truck or platform truck cart.

  - ○ Holds at least 100 lbs.

  - ○ Collapsible and fits in your vehicle.

  - ○ Rubber wheels for parking lots and floors.

You might have noticed I didn't mention a laptop. A laptop is extra weight to carry, and another distraction from noticing the readers who wander by your booth when you aren't looking. I take mine to every event, and never pull it out of the computer bag. I think it's my emotional support animal.

There is a typical lull time from 1:30 until 3:00, but I take advantage of the break and visit with neighbors or sit down for a little people-watching and some water.

Where to Scale Back

If you have to scale back, leave behind extra tables, display racks, and any other bulky items.

Do you have too many books? Double- check to be sure you didn't sneak in extras that aren't on your list. If your count is good, put the extra bin you do want to take on the back seat or rearrange to make room.

Event Buddy

Events are easier to manage if someone goes with you, especially if they are strong enough to help you put up and take down your tent (outdoor events) and carry or haul books, tables, etc. and big bonus if they will handle the sales for you too so you can focus on your readers and sign books!

My Event Buddy is my husband. We were at an event last year, and as usual, he and the neighbor next to us chatted.

He told her I was Management, and he was Labor. It definitely tickled her funny bone, because she repeated it to everyone who visited her booth.

It was surprising because after they bought items from her, her customers frequently bought a book or even three from us and joked with Labor when he put their books into a sack.

Tip: Serendipity happens. Your vendor neighbor might be your best marketer.

Setup Rules

Respect the event rules when you set up. In fact, have the event requirements printed or handy on your phone as a reminder of their rules because every event is different.

Outdoor events assign spaces that are frequently 10ft x 10ft or occasionally 12ft by 12ft. Some events have rules that specifically restrict the vendor from having any items outside of their assigned 10ft x 10ft spot, and others are more lenient. It's important to know the event rules in advance, but you can observe returning vendors to see how tightly the rules are enforced.

Indoor events spaces are also frequently 10ft x 10ft or 8ft x 10ft. Indoor events are more likely to provide tables and sell full tables and half tables. Their event fees tend to be more expensive, so a half table is perfect for an author with fewer books.

OUTDOOR SETUP EXAMPLE

Tent is set up for readers to stop and browse at the front or back

Canopy Tent with an Author banner across the front. Same Author banner is also on the back.

There are 50 Books (7 series and an omnibus) on the front table. Our assigned spot was in the middle of the road, so the tables on the "back" side of the tent duplicates the front tables. I love two-way festival traffic, but an Event Buddy is definitely critical to help with sales when readers show up at the two tables.

Can you tell there is no access for us to get out from behind our tables? We had to either move a table for a restroom break (crawl under a table?) or rely on the kindness of our neighbors to allow us to slip out through their tent space. We've been fortunate to have friendly neighbors, and we are always careful to limit our trespassing.

INDOOR SETUP EXAMPLE

Best possible set up. Readers can browse on any of the three open sides.

Indoor table with the Author tent banner serving as a table banner.

This is an example of an indoor setup. There are 40 books (5 series and an omnibus) on the front table. The table along the open side is Table #2 and duplicates the books on Table #1.

Tip: The tent banner has become a table banner courtesy of heavy duty tape. Also, I could have hung the banner from the pipe and draping with three pants hangers that we clipped to the banner and then hung from the pipe.

The neighbor on one side of me was a no-show, and I had a walkway on the other side, so that third table was where I put trilogies. This is the best spot I've ever had, and the sales showed it.

I wish I could figure out how to request a corner location with a no-show neighbor.

Going Solo

Solo vending is absolutely doable, but it will take extra planning. Keep your display compact. The fewer parts you have to manage, the faster setup and teardown will be.

All the vendors I've asked to watch my booth when I was solo while I dashed to the restroom were more than willing. Make sure your cash box is locked and hidden.

Solo Outdoor Event: The Canopy Tent

If it's an outdoor event and you'll be at the event solo, you will need help with your tent. The best case is if someone who is experienced goes with you to set up then returns before the end of the event for takedown.

If you're solo, your vending neighbors may lend a hand for set up, but you will need to tell them what to do because not all tents are the same. When it's time to leave, you may have to take the tent down by yourself because everyone will be rushed to go home.

Tip: Practice, practice, practice with your tent until you are completely clear on what you can do and what you need the other person to do, and how to close up your tent alone, if you have to.

Books and Inventory

How Many Books?

This is the question every author asks, and I have an answer! You want enough books so you don't run out, but not more books than you can unload from your vehicle to your event site in less than thirty minutes.

Single Book

If you currently have only one published book, take 15-20 books and cover one table with them.

Series of Books

If you have a series, here's a general rule of thumb:
For EACH series:
Book 1: 12 copies
Book 2: 4 copies
Book 3: 4 copies
Books 4 thru Book Last: 2 copies each
You'll have enough books to sell
- Two complete series

- Two trilogies

- Eight Book 1s as singles

Tip: Pack a PANIC bin, which is a bin you leave in your vehicle with one of all your books except include a second copy of your Book 1s. I've actually had to send my Event Buddy to grab a book or two from the PANIC bin.

Book Setup

On the table facing the foot traffic, put all the books for each series in a stack with the spines toward the readers, then put one Book 1 in front of the stack for readers to pick up. If you have room, add trilogies.

If you have a second table, duplicate the first table.

If you've filled both tables because you have so many series, it's time to think about a third or even fourth table with wire table racks, especially if you have a third side where readers can browse.

As your number of books grows, look at your sales and the cost of a second booth. It might be time to expand to two booths with more tables for your books. (Yay!)

If you're restricted to one table and have too many series to get all of them on the table with your usual set up, either pick the series you want to highlight for that event, or practice on a table at home to see how you want to set up the books.

If you have a half-table at an event, pick your top two or three series to take, but take the rest and leave them in your car because your neighbor might be a no-show.

STORING BOOKS BETWEEN EVENTS

If you're going to schedule more than one event a year, you'll need a plan to store your books separate from your home inventory so you don't have to repack your bins for every event.

Avoid moisture, heat, and any place your cat might decide is its new scratchpad or your puppy can discover its new chew toy.

Storage Basics

- Select sturdy, stackable plastic totes with tight lids. Uniform size is a must.

- Store books in a closet or use under-bed bins.

- If you have room, store books in your office.

- You could store books in your garage, if the bins are not directly on the floor, but ONLY if you live in an arid region. Books need a warning sign: Humidity Kills.

Label your bins with what's inside, so you're not rummaging at the last minute. For example, my bins are labeled by series name and which table, by number or 'name', they will go on at the event. I label Table #1 'Table', and Table #2 'Backup'. My PANIC bins are labeled by series, and yes, they are actually labeled PANIC bin.

Tip: Don't load your books into the biggest bin you can find. The maximum number of books in a bin I can pick up from the floor repeatedly without injuring myself is 20, so the plastic bins we use have a maximum capacity of 20 books.

MY BINS READY TO GO

All the books are ready to load in the 15 bins.

If you look closely, you'll see tablecloths and other items to go on the tables which simplifies loading and unloading.

Can you believe I have two spare bins? They won't be spares for long.

ORDERING BOOKS

Allow plenty of lead time when you order print-on-demand books. Print delays happen, and always at the worst possible time. For most authors, a three week buffer is okay, but a four week buffer is better.

When to Reorder More Books

When you return home, unload your bins of books from your vehicle immediately. You can unload everything else the next day.

One or two days after you return home, inventory your bins and replenish them from the books you have stored at home for the next event.

As you replenish books in your bins from your home storage, verify the number of books you have left in your home storage. Check your event schedule for the next three months, and order more author copies to have enough books in your home storage for the upcoming events.

Chapter 3: Event Logistics

PLANNING YOUR DAY

The secret to a low-stress event day? I have no clue. I'm a frantic mess until after I'm completely set up and ready for readers.

However, I still have a plan. I know when to arrive, what to bring, and the order to unload. We can put up our tent for an outdoor event with the tent weights and the tent banner in place, and our tables unfolded and ready for tablecloths in less than fifteen minutes.

After we've unloaded everything at our site and the tent and tables are ready, I become random. Each setup is a little different that the one before, and I have to "see" different setups before I can decide how we'll set up for this once again unique assigned spot. My final set up takes an hour or more.

A No-Show Neighbor

Butterflies on stilts are showing you Table #2

My neighbor didn't show up, but butterflies on stilts came to help me show off at my booth.

My neighbor was a no-show, so my Table #2 was on a side next to the front. The event didn't restrict vendors to their 10ft x 10ft canopy, so I put my A-frame sandwich board sign near the corner of my tent.

The A-frame sign says 'Meet the Author' with a photo of me and a collage of a bunch of my books on one side and 'Signed by the Author' with the same photo and collage on the other side.

Butterflies on stilts flitted by then stopped to pose with me at my booth. You know what they say, if there isn't a photo, it didn't happen. Also, if we aren't having fun, why are we even doing this?

Know Your Timeline

Arrival Time

Most events offer a one to two-hour vendor setup window the day of the event. Arrive as early as possible for setup, especially if it's your first time at this event.

Some events will allow you to drop off items the day before the event starts. The advantage of the early setup is you'll see your site, but if it's an outdoor event, don't leave your books and take two towels with you the morning of the event to dry off your tables because dew happens.

Tip: *Outdoor*: If you're arriving while it's still dark, which is most of the time for us, have a flashlight and a battery powered light you can hang on your tent during setup.

Tripping over something in the dark and falling on concrete is not fun. (Don't ask.)

Setup Time

Plan on an hour to set up; longer for your first several times attending events until you have smoothed out your system.

SURFACE AND TERRAIN: OUTDOOR EVENTS

Surface and terrain are frequently the biggest variables.

Your assigned spot on a street may have a huge difference between the low spot next to the curb and the high spot where the street has a curved peak in the middle. You may have to use blocks of wood to raise the back of the tent to make it higher, or you may have to lower the front with one click on both legs of the tent.

If your spot is on grass or the side of a hill, you'll have to adjust one side or the other.

If your choice is to have an uneven, cockeyed tent or a tent so low that you or your Event Buddy can't stand up without bumping a head, go for the uneven tent.

GETTING TO YOUR SPOT: INDOOR EVENTS

Scope out the best way to get from the parking lot to the door so you aren't trying to jump a curb.

Tip: Park near the restricted parking spots if you can. They frequently have cuts in the curb for wheelchairs.

If your spot is not on the same level as the entrance, you'll be juggling time in the elevator along with everyone else to get to your floor, which is another reason to go early and to allow extra time for setup.

EVENT DURATION

Know what time your event starts and when it's over. You must be ready to sell before the event starts.

Tip: Vendors frequently like to browse thirty minutes before the event opens. Be ready for surprise early sales. (Yay!)

The rules for most events specify you cannot leave before a specified time. Some allow a soft breakdown; others don't. Know the rules of your event. Don't do a soft breakdown just because someone else is. They might have special permission to leave early.

Soft Breakdown

Soft breakdown means your booth still looks open for business, and is not half stripped. A soft breakdown allows you to pack up and your Event Budy to take parts of your display and products to your vehicle, but you must still have enough of your display and products left to entice passersby to stop and buy books.

This strategy works best if you've parked relatively close and your Event Buddy can make trips on foot with a cart.

If your vehicle is too far away or the terrain is not acceptable, for example, you'd have to cross four lanes of busy traffic, you will have to wait to bring your vehicle to your spot to load up. You can pack the bins that are still stored at your booth until it's time to leave.

Tip: A wagon, cart, or hand truck is critical for a soft breakdown.

Teardown

Don't completely shut down your store before the end of the event, but when it's time to leave, at least half of your inventory should be packed and ready to go. Expect your teardown to take thirty to sixty minutes. You'll become more efficient as you attend more events.

Moving In and Out

Unloading at the Event

You will either have received instructions from the event organizer before event day, or you'll receive instructions when you sign in.

Most of the time, you'll be allowed to drive to your assigned spot for an outdoor event, which is another good reason to arrive as early as you can.

For an indoor event, you may be allowed to park at the entrance, unload, and then move your vehicle. The closer it gets to the time for the event to start, the more chaotic it becomes.

Park as close to your assigned spot or the closest entrance to your assigned spot as you can and unload everything then move your car immediately, not only to clear the way for others but also to keep from getting blocked in. Volunteers are occasionally available to help you unload, but don't count on it.

There may be an assigned vendor lot for parking. Be strategic about where you park. You want to be relatively close to your site, but you also want to have a clear idea of how you will leave.

Tip: Don't park illegally in a no parking zone or in business lots that have been identified as off limits. You'll be ticketed and towed, and your day will be ruined.

Loading Up to Leave

You may or may not be allowed to drive your vehicle to your spot (outdoor) or the entrance (indoor) to load up. If you are, assess whether it would be simpler to load a wagon and take everything to your vehicle, even if it means several trips, especially if you began with a soft breakdown.

Terrain and limited exits can make or break your set up and take down strategy, but you've probably already figured that out.

Tip: Scope out the terrain or entrances if it's a new-to-you event. Look at maps or photos online or ask any returning vendors what the setup area is like.

Packing Order

- Pack up your books first.

- Fold and secure signs and banners before collapsing your tables. Outdoor: then your tent.

- Double-check for small items: your card reader, hand sanitizer, pens.

- Leave your space cleaner than you found it. I always bring a trash sack so I don't have to go hunting for a trash bin to throw something away.

Don't rush; be methodical. Everyone's tired.

FINAL THOUGHTS ON LOGISTICS

Event day doesn't have to be chaotic. Show up early, bring what you need, and treat setup and teardown like part of your process not an afterthought. The smoother your logistics, the more energy you'll have to engage with readers.

Chapter 4: Personal Prep and Comfort

You've packed your books, your banners, your pricing signs—but what about *you*? Events where you sell your books can be fun, but they're also physically demanding. The more you care for yourself, the better you'll sell.

DRESS FOR THE DAY

Dress like you're ready to work but approachable and in line with your book's vibe. See Chapter Ten for the more event-targeted suggestions for style.

STYLE GUIDELINES

- Look like the author you are. Wear something that identifies you as an author or that makes you feel like an author. Even though I wear my author T-shirt with my logo and my. author ball cap, I still get asked, "Are you the author?" But that's okay because the reader is engaged.

- Prioritize comfort. Wear comfortable shoes and comfortable clothing. You'll be standing, sitting, bending, and walking.

- Layers make a difference. Mornings may start cold and afternoons may be hot, cold, or rainy (hopefully it doesn't rain indoors, but roof leaks happen. Ask me how I know.) A lightweight long-sleeved shirt or jacket can be a lifesaver.

- Change of clothes. I always have a change of clothes. I once spilled a full cup of cold coffee on my shirt. I was glad I had a change with me.

Outdoor: Hat, Sunglasses, and Protection

For outdoor events, prepare like you're going camping for the day. Shade and sun protection are essential.

- A wide-brimmed hat or ball cap.

- Sunglasses.

- Sunscreen.

- Bug spray for those early morning or evening setups.

Bonus: Branded hats with your logo or genre can double as advertising.

Staying Comfortable

It's amazing how fast you can become tired, overheated, or dehydrated if you're not paying attention. Pack the basics and lunch and remember to stay hydrated.

The Basics

- A thermos of hot coffee or tea to get you through the morning.

- A cushion or chair pad for long sitting spells.

- Water.

- Snacks you can eat quickly: protein bars, trail mix, crackers.

- Hand wipes or baby wipes.

- Mini first-aid kit.

- Small pack of tissues. You'll see why when you go to your first outdoor event.

LUNCH

Food from food trucks is my favorite, but standing in a line and waiting to order is not possible.

- Pack your own lunch: sandwich, fruit, and a cookie or treat.

- Pack hot soup in a thermos when the weather's cold and thank me later. Don't forget spoons and napkins.

- Pack your lunch and drinks in a small cooler or insulated lunch bag.

- Eat when you can. It might be a bite here and there.

- Plan on eating before noon or after two. It's been my experience that we are busiest between 11:30 and 1:30. I can't explain it.

Stay Hydrated

Dehydration is exhausting, and it's harder to recover once it sets in.

- Bring a large reusable water bottle or thermos.

- Keep a second smaller bottle of water within easy reach on the table.

End-of-Day Recovery

Spending an entire day on your feet and talking to people is exhausting. Hydrate on the way home.

You'll have to unload your books, but leave everything else for the next day.

Plan a light, easy-to-fix meal for the evening and enjoy collapsing. You've earned it.

Chapter 5: Your Booth

Your booth is your storefront. It's what people see before they ever hear a word from you. A great setup doesn't have to be expensive or elaborate to be inviting, and easy to browse.

YOUR CANOPY TENT

Outdoors Only

- Sturdy frame that is steel or reinforced aluminum, not plastic.

- Straight legs are better because you lose space with angled legs on a tent.

- Weights on all four legs of the tent are *essential* for safety and are frequently required by events.

- Accessories for the tent: binder clips,

bungee cords, and long zip ties to secure the tent banners to the tent legs.

- Tent stakes are frequently mentioned, but you're better off with weights. Organizers frequently do not allow tent stakes.

Tip: If you're borrowing a tent or have bought a new tent test setup at home first to be sure all the pieces are there and you know how to set it up.

Tables and Layout

We have three 6-foot folding tables and one 4-foot folding table. We frequently use two 6-ft tables to make an L across the front, so I have room to get in and out. Our 4-ft table is our "floater." It goes in different places, depending on what we find when we set up.

My ideal goal is to have two sides of my space, front and back, or front and one side, so there is room for more than one reader to look at all the books at once. Remember, Table #1 and Table #2 are duplicates.

I've noticed that readers are often hesitant to approach a table if another person is already browsing. They'll often pause at a distance then move on, which is why having multiple points of access to your books can be so effective.

We've frequently had sales from the two sides simultaneously when people have their own space to browse.

Do you have to do that? No, but maybe you'd like to test it out sometime. Your layout should allow people to approach comfortably, see everything at a glance, and browse without feeling crowded.

Layout: "They Say" and Tips

- They Say: Place books at different heights; use risers, boxes under cloths, or shelves.

- Tip: You already have different heights with your stack of series behind your single Book 1. All the books invite being picked up. You don't want your books to be in a neat untouchable "display." The one exception is foldable metal racks. They're excellent at showing off your trilogies.

- They Say: Stand in front of your table so you can engage with your reader.

- Tip: Never stand between your reader and

your books. Stay behind your table and out of the way. Leave room to stand behind.

- They Say: Don't clutter your table. Leaving space between your featured titles looks more open and inviting than everything crammed together.

- Tip: Neat stacks of books by series allow you to put all of your series on the front table. Drop business cards on your front table in three different places so readers can snag a business card to remember you if that's what they want to do. They are likely to check out your website, pick a book and order it, and subscribe to the newsletter. I always have a boost of orders on my book shop and the retailers and new subscribers after all the events.

TABLE GEAR

- They Say: Use Tablecloth(s) that are floor-length to hide your supplies underneath. Stretchy tablecloths that stretch over the legs are elegant and look more professional.

- Tip: Outdoor: Longish regular tablecloth is fine. Floor-length will get dirty. The wind blows the tablecloths and allows the bins underneath to show, but readers are focused on your books. The stretchy leg tablecloths don't blow, but they do become dirty in grass and dirt.

- Tip: Indoor: Floor-length tablecloths to hide bins may be an event requirement. The cheaper stretchy, made-to-fit tablecloths stretch out after a few seasons. Consider investing in quality tablecloths for indoor events.

- They Say: *Outdoor* Clip-on or weighted edges for outdoor use to keep your tablecloth from blowing.

- Tip: The wind blows outdoor tablecloths, but you have books on top of the tablecloth. However, book covers curl when the wind blows them, so I have a bucket of river rocks to put on my books. Bonus: people love to feel the smoothness of the rocks. Some people will even rearrange them. Then, they buy a book.

Tip: A **tall director's chair** lets you sit without vanishing behind your books. When I sit down in a regular camping chair, you can't see me, but it actually doesn't matter because I stand nearly all the time.

Tip: Flat, **interlocking floor mats** are perfect to stand on for 7-9 hours, particularly when your spot is on a hard surface.

Tip: **Clear, heavy duty shower curtains** are perfect to toss over your books on a table when a stray shower or a downpour, including a roof leak, comes out of nowhere.

Two-Day **Indoor** Tip: If you leave your books on the table overnight, cover your books with old sheets or shower curtains. You won't have to set up again the next day, but there's no temptation for someone to "borrow" a book on their way out.

BRANDING AND SIGNAGE

My goal is for people to know at a glance I am the author and my product is fiction books with crime, mystery, and thriller stories. They instantly realize how much the books are and why buying three or more is a bargain.

Banners, Flags, and Signs

- Must Have: **Price sign** especially if you offer discounts. I design my price signs using online graphic design tools and print them on 8.5in x 11in paper and slip the sheet into a sign holder. Keep it clear, large, and legible. List prices for 1 book, 2 books, 3 books, etc. My discounts start with 3 books. I have two sign holders that are adjustable. I put them on the back table and a side table. Prices are no surprise. It's interesting watching people trying to decide which three books they want so they can get them at a bargain price.

- Must Have: **Author sign** signifies the vendor is the author. Your name along with your picture, genre(s), logo, or "Local Author."

- Nice to Have: **Tent or Table Banner.** I have two tent banners that are exactly alike, so I can put one on the front and one where Table #2 is. Author name, genres, website. My banners also double as table banners with the help of heavy duty tape.

- Nice to Have: **Series Signs.** I have 'menu holders' for 4in x 6in cards with the name of the series and a photo with all the books in the series. I put the series menu holder on top of the stack of the series. Bonus: they keep the covers from being blown by the wind.

- Nice to have: **A-frame plastic sign** with "Meet the Author" on one side and "Author Book Signing" on the other side. It includes my photo and a collage of some of my paperbacks. The signs are legible from ten feet away.

COMFORT GEAR

If you're at an outdoor event, you will be standing for hours in the heat, cold, or wind, or all three in one day.

We attended an indoor event with an air conditioning system that couldn't keep up with the afternoon heat and the number of people in the building.

Tip: Have a fan available for an indoor event when the weather is warm.

- **Fans.**

  - Shop fan, battery powered. We have two.

  - Outdoor: Tent ceiling fan with built in battery charged by USB. Tip: invite an overheated neighbor to sit under the fan to cool off.

- **Outdoor Portable Heater.**

  - Camper-style.

  - Spare fuel canister.

Chapter 6: Branding Materials

Your brand is your identity as a writer and how your readers see and perceive you. When people walk away from your booth, they should remember *you*, not just the book they bought.

WHAT IS YOUR BRAND?

Not sure what your brand is? Here are some questions for you to answer that will help you.

IDENTIFY YOUR NICHE

Identifying your niche helps readers recognize you, and it helps you focus on your marketing efforts.

- What genres do I consistently write in?

- What recurring themes, moods, or character types show up in my stories?

- What emotional or imaginative experience do readers consistently get from my books?

Determine Your Unique Value Proposition (UVP)

According to Shopify, a strong UVP gives potential customers three key insights.

1. What your product provides.

2. Why they need it.

3. How your offering differs from competitors.

Write your UVP by answering the following question.

- What makes your voice or approach different from others writing in your genre?

- What do readers say they love most about your books?

- Are you especially good at plot twists, humor, world-building, emotional depth, or something else?

Develop a Tagline with a Clear Message

Use your tagline consistently on your website, bookmarks, banners, emails, and book signings. It becomes shorthand for who you are as an author. My tagline is splashed everywhere.

Test the message of your tagline.

- Is it a brief, single sentence?

- Is it reflective of your personality and writing style?

- Does it convey a promise to your reader?

Establish Your Brand Story

A strong brand story creates emotional resonance. People remember stories, especially the one that brought you here.

Your brand story includes

- Why you started writing.

- What keeps you going.

- What makes your writing journey different.

Pulling it All Together

Your brand starts with how your books feel at a glance. What do readers feel when they see your covers? Warm and fuzzy from pastels? Intrigue from dark and gritty tones? Whimsical vibes from jewel-toned colors?

This "look and feel" should match your display materials and giveaways.

Your Brand, at a Minimum

- A logo even if it's just your name in a consistent font.

- A tagline or one-sentence hook.

- Similar colors across signs, banners, and marketing items.

What Your Brand Communicates

- Genre (s) or overall theme.

- A promise of the tone of your books. Funny, romantic, suspenseful, spicy, low spice, etc.

- Professionalism.

- A sense of "you" as the author behind the books.

Pro Tip: If you have multiple genres, consider developing a theme for your author brand or use your business as an umbrella that covers all the pieces in your author brand.

Your Logo and Tagline

Your **Logo** can be a stylized version of your name, initials, or author photo with a symbol. Think clean, readable, and reproducible in black and white. Use the same logo on your banner, business cards, website, and book bags.

Since your **Tagline** is your promise to your readers, use it on your banner, business cards, and your website.

Branded Packaging

Branded bags and packaging take your booth from amateur to professional in one easy step. When someone walks away holding a bag with your name on it, you've just created free advertising for the rest of the event.

I use book-sized brown paper sacks with handles and add stickers with my logo, tagline, and website to both sides. We prep the sacks before an event.

Business Cards

Keep these easily accessible on your table. I used to use a business card holder. It was pretty, but not practical.

Now I drop cards on the table so they are easy for anyone to pick up.

- Your author name and tagline.

- Logo.

- Website.

- Email or social handle.

- QR code linking to your website, newsletter sign-up, or store.

I recommend printing on both sides of your business cards.

Print one side with your author website, email, and QR code for your newsletter.

Print the other side with your online shop logo, website, email, and QR code.

Your business card is your best marketing tool at the event for your online shop.

You have an interested reader standing in front of you. Leverage the momentum of your in-person connection and have them turn the card to the side with your online shop.

"You can buy more books from me on my online shop. I have all my books there as paperbacks, eBooks, and audiobooks. And I have discounts and bargains you won't find anywhere else."

If you don't have an online shop, the second side could be your author photo and bio, list of series, social media handles, or whatever you'd like to highlight.

Bookmarks, Postcards, Character Cards

Bookmarks, postcards, and character cards are frequently considered "swag" and are given away in the book events and conventions worlds.

In the craft festival world, bookmarks, postcards, and character cards are bonuses for a purchase. We preload each sack with them before the event.

NEWSLETTER SIGN-UP WITH QR CODE

A sale is not our final goal; it's just the start. What we really want is a long-term reader. That's where the newsletter email list comes in.

- Clearly display a sign on your table with the QR code that links to your sign-up form landing page.

- Some people are QR code leery. Include the URL to your landing page on your sign.

- You may want to keep a clipboard sign-up sheet handy. Some people still want to sign up for a newsletter on paper and not fiddle with their phone. Tip: Before they get away, read their email address to them because sometimes what they wrote is hard to decipher later.

Tip: Position your newsletter sign-up with the QR code away from the checkout area so people can take a quick snap and run away. (Yes, they do that.)

Your Website: Your Digital Home Base

After the event or even during the event, readers may want to look you up. Your website should reflect the same vibe and branding as your booth.

- An easy-to-remember URL. Your author name is best, if possible. Mine is judithabarrett dot com.

- Book covers, blurbs, and buy links to your online shop or a single URL that directs the reader to their preferred retailer. The books on my author website point to my online book shop, which is BarrettBookShop dot com.

- Newsletter sign-up link.

- Blog is optional, but it's another channel to reach readers. I'm prejudiced because I have blogged for years and like it. Don't start blogging if it seems like another chore.

Use your website as a hub to point readers where they can buy your book. Most authors use a link that directs the reader to their preferred retailer.

While I use the links to my online shop, I've discovered readers who have a retailer preference will go to the retailer to buy the book they found on my website. They don't need a link, and some people are becoming leery of online links.

Chapter 7: Marketing

You've signed up for the event, your inventory is ready, and you're dreaming of a bustling booth full of happy readers. But before any of that can happen, people need to know you'll be there.

While the event organizers frequently advertise, it's rarely enough to guarantee your ideal audience will show up at your booth. The purpose of your marketing efforts is to roll out the welcome mat for your loyal readers and the readers who haven't met you yet.

KNOW THE EVENT, KNOW THE AUDIENCE

Start by understanding who the event attracts so you can tailor your message. A fine art festival may have a different vibe than a craft fair or a downtown market day.

Tip: Ask the organizers for any promotional materials you can share, like event graphics, hashtags, or their social media handles. Many will even repost your promotional posts if you tag them.

START EARLY TO BUILD ANTICIPATION

Begin spreading the word about four to six weeks before the event to give the readers time to adjust their schedule. Event goers who plan their weekends in advance will appreciate advance notice.

Create a simple promotional calendar

- 4 weeks out: Announce the event.

- 2–3 weeks out: Share behind-the-scenes prep.

- 1 week out: Post a reminder and tease what you're bringing.

- Day of the event: Post a "come see me!" message with a booth photo.

- After the event: Share photos and thank your readers who came.

Your Newsletter

Your newsletter subscribers are your most loyal readers. Let them know where you'll be and why they should come. A warm, friendly message can go a long way.

SAMPLE NEWSLETTER ANNOUNCEMENT

"I'll be at the Sweet Magnolia Festival on Saturday, July 12 from 10 to 4, with all my paperbacks, book totes, and a few unique surprises. Stop by and say hello; if you mention this email, I have a little something for you!"

You can also share fun prep moments with your subscribers as you choose which books to bring, pack your bins, or decide on your table setup. Readers love seeing the behind-the-scenes process.

SOCIAL MEDIA: YOUR ONGOING BILLBOARD

Whether you're active on Facebook, Instagram, X, Pinterest, or TikTok, your social media platforms are excellent tools for reaching readers and locals who follow you.

What to Post

- Countdown graphics, for example, "3 weeks until the Book & Craft Fair!"

- Sneak peeks of what you're taking to the event.

- Packing or setup videos.

- Shout-outs to fellow vendors or the event itself.

- Day-of the event booth photos and event highlights.

Boost Visibility
- Using the event's hashtag.

- Tagging the event page.

- Sharing your location on stories on the day of the event.

It's okay to talk about the same event more than once because social media is fast-moving, and repetition helps.

Blogging: The Long Game

If you keep a blog on your author site, write a post about why you're excited about the event. Mention what makes this event special and how readers can find your booth. If it's a recurring event, share highlights or photos from previous years.

These posts are helpful for readers and boost your website's search visibility too.

Cross-Promotion with Other Creators

Are other authors or friends attending the event? Share each other's posts and cheer each other on. You can even run a joint giveaway, like a free tote bag drawing for visitors who stop by all the booths of the authors who are taking part in the giveaway.

Tip: It makes the event more fun when you have a team vibe going.

Local Promotions That Still Work

- Submit the event to local event calendars online.

- Post flyers in your local library, bookstore, or favorite coffee shop.

- Ask to be featured on the event's Facebook or Instagram page. They often highlight vendors in the days leading up to the event.

During the Event: Show You're There

Let people know you've arrived! A booth selfie or quick video saying "Come visit me today!" can tip a reader into their car.

What to Post

- Photos of your setup.

- Reader selfies (with permission).

- Popular items or what's selling fast.

Tag the event and use local hashtags to catch the eye of folks already at the festival.

After the Event: Keep the Momentum Going

After you're home and unpacked, don't go quiet. Thank your readers online and in your newsletter. Share a few highlights or funny moments. Let people know how much their support meant and give them a hint about your next event.

These post-event touches keep readers engaged between appearances and build loyalty.

Quick Marketing Checklist

Before the Event

- Announce event in newsletter and on social media.

- Share countdowns or behind-the-scenes prep.

- Submit to local calendars or community boards.

- Coordinate with fellow vendors for cross-promotion.

DURING THE EVENT

- Post booth photos and location.

- Use event hashtags and tag organizers.

- Share stories or reels.

- Take photos for future use.

AFTER THE EVENT

- Thank attendees.

- Share event highlights.

- Mention next event or link to your online shop.

TAKE A BREATH

Marketing your event appearances doesn't have to be overwhelming. Pick a few tools that suit your style, and be consistent. Your goal is to connect with readers, old and new, and invite them to share your bookish world.

Let your enthusiasm lead the way. If you're excited, your readers will be too.

Chapter 8: Pricing and Payments

Finally, we're going to talk about money.

Pricing can make or break your event experience. If the price is too high, readers walk away. But it's not all bad if a few people walk away because there's the possibility they may have been only browsers and not serious readers.

If the price is too low, you lose profit and cheapen the value of your work. This chapter is all about finding that sweet spot and making it easy for readers to say "yes."

SETTING YOUR PRICES

Let's start with the big question: How much should I charge for my books?

There are many ways to determine the price of books. Here is a suggestion to give you some ideas.

Retail vs. Direct Sales

- **Retailers:** The price you have set for the retailers should be the highest cost for your paperback.

- **Direct Sales:** If the price for the same paperback you sell in person should be less than retail, how much less? That's next!

Your Price for Direct, In-Person Sales

Check the Market

Similar Products

The logical assumption would be to check similar products at the same events to see what those vendors are charging. You see the problem with that, right? How do you know what the authors are selling their books for before you're at the event?

If preorders for books are available for the event you'll be attending, check the preorders; or if you know an author who regularly sells at events, ask them what the typical prices are.

For craft fairs, I'm frequently the only vendor selling books, so I came up with a frequently sold product for comparison. I got the idea four years ago from a talented vendor who was selling her products like crazy at the booth next to me. In fact, she sent business to me. "Now that you've bought a T-shirt, go buy a book. You deserve it." And they did!

Coincidentally, my books were priced at the same price as her T-shirts, which was her inspiration, and made bells go off in my head. My books were a product match for quality T-shirts at an arts and crafts fair!

Last year, vendors who sold T-shirts that were the same quality as her T-shirts quietly raised their prices. I watched at several events, and quality T-shirt sales didn't drop, so I did the same.

Are you still with me? Do your own math and keep an eye on the prices of quality products at events.

OUR FINAL PRICE

Price your books in line with a quality product similar to yours, but keep your price above your breakeven cost.

You might have to be a little creative to find a similar quality product, but we're authors, so creativity is our superpower.

A tip: Remember our rule that retail is the highest price? We may have to raise our retail price before we go to the event.

Readers do check retailer prices all the time while they're standing at my booth. They think they're being sneaky, but I let them comparison shop because I never come out on the short end.

Think about it: what if they could buy your paperback from their favorite retailer for $1.00 less than they are paying to buy it from you?

Yes, you'll sign your book, but is your signature worth $1.00 to that reader? That's not what I want my reader to be thinking about. Don't make them struggle with that decision.

Price the retailer to give your reader the satisfaction of the bargain of a book that's cheaper than retail by even $1.00. PLUS when they buy from you, their book includes the author's signature, and they are supporting a local author!

Tip: Please don't be afraid to charge what your book is worth. You're a vendor, and you are at the event in person to make money.

How To Price Your Book

Cost of One Paperback

Calculate the average cost of an author copy of your paperback by dividing the total cost of your order of paperback books, which includes the printing and shipping, by the number of books you ordered.

Expected or Average Number of Books Sold at an Event

How many books do you expect to sell at an event? If you have no history to fall back on, go with your best guess. If you have an author friend or you're in an author group with an author or two who sells books similar to yours at events, ask them how many books they typically sell. Adjust their number for you if they are more experienced.

Event Registration Fee

Divide the event registration fee by the number of books you expect to sell at the event.

One Paperback's Cost Per Event including fuel

The other significant expense for an event is fuel. There are so many variables for fuel like distance to and from the event and the average miles per gallon of your vehicle, but we'll start with your best guess estimate based on your typical costs for fuel.

Total Basic Cost per Book per Event with fuel costs added

Our total basic cost per book per event is the cost of a book + one book's share of the event fee + one book's share of the fuel cost = total basic cost of one book for the event.

Price Example with Numbers

Here's an example with numbers, if seeing the numbers helps you. Note: the numbers are only to show the math; they aren't realistic.

- Cost of your 5 shipped books $50

- Cost of 1 book (50/5) **$10**

- Number of books expected to be sold **6**

- Event registration fee $18

- Cost of the event per book (18/6) **$3**

- Cost of fuel $24

- Cost of fuel per book (24/6) **$4**

- Total cost of one book for the event $10 + $3 + $4 = $17

It's your turn to do your math. (Remember, the above numbers show math, not real data.)

Now we have an estimate that helps us know we how much we have to charge to break even, but we're vendors, so just breaking even is not our goal. Let's move on to pricing our book.

Volume Discounts

Nothing boosts your sales like bundling. The average person might hesitate to buy one book, but if you give them a deal if they buy two or more books, you've instantly made a friend and a fan.

A Bundling Example

- 1 Book $20

- 2 Books $40

- 3 Books $55

- 4 Books $70

- 5 Books $85

- 6 Books $100

Bundling works not only with series, but surprisingly, some of my creative readers have decided they'd like to try three different Book 1s! I've had more than one reader decide to bundle Book 1s from 5 different series so they can decide which series they want to read first.

I don't have to push bundling because readers study the price sign. (I love readers.)

My only exception is when a reader wants to buy two books, I casually mention they could get one more book for $15, which saves them $10.

Everybody likes to save $10.

Cash and Cards

Cash

Some readers bring cash to events to manage their spending. The cash buyers are why my books are priced in numbers divided by five. I discount the book for cash buyers by paying the sales tax for them so we don't have to make change in coins. Each state has different rules on how a vendor can do that. Check your state's tax rules.

Keep your cash box handy so you can make change, but out of sight because you don't want to flash your cash stash. If your bills are stored in slots by denominations, making change will be easier.

Cards

Charge and debit cards are the most common way people pay for products at events.

- Card reader apps collect payment from credit and debit cards in person. Many vendors use Square.

- Card readers can use data mode with Wi-Fi or you may have to switch to your phone's hot spot if Wi-Fi at the event is slowed by everyone using it.

- Apps support tap to pay with your smartphone, but some cards require a card reader.

Test your card reader and the app before you leave home and onsite before the event. Nothing is worse than fumbling while someone's ready to buy.

Tip: Have a power bank in case the phone battery runs low.

Final Thoughts on Pricing & Payments

I don't mention price unless they ask. My price signs are very eye-catching and easy to read.

However, when they ask, "How much is this book?" I'll tell them, and most of the time they point to the sign and laugh. "Oh yes, it's right there." I don't know why people do that, but it's very common.

I do suggest one more book if they tell me they want "These two."

When they say "I'll take these," I ask, "Cash or charge?" We have moved past the decision point of whether they'll buy the books to determining how they want to pay for them.

Tip: If they are paying with a credit card, I wait until the Hubs says the card is approved before I write their name in the book. I'm a master at gathering my pen and opening to the right page.

Never apologize for your prices. You are offering a professionally written, edited, and produced product. Be proud of it.

If they say anything like "that's too much" or "I can buy a book at the library for $5", smile and nod. **They are not your reader, which is no reflection on you.**

Selling books isn't about "getting money out of people." It's about having stories readers love and making it fun for them to buy it from you.

When you connect authentically and confidently with people who are browsing, the sales will follow.

Chapter 9: Customer Interaction

First Impressions Count

There's a fine line between welcoming and hovering. People want to browse without pressure, but they don't want to be ignored. Find the sweet spot and strike that balance.

My Greeting Strategy

- I watch them as they approach my table and smile.

- I stay quiet while they look over the covers before I ask, "What do you like to read?"

- I listen to what they say.

- I'm really low key, but that's me. I'm

interested in learning what they like so I can help them find a book and a series they will love.

Your Greeting Strategy

- Make eye contact and smile.

- Develop your own strategy because you will be more natural, and that's what draws people to you.

My Book Pitch

- "Which cover caught your eye? Pick up the book and read the back to see what the book's about." Why: They'll pick up the book that interested them. They've gone from seeing to touching.

- I stay quiet and watch them while they read and become immersed in the character and story. Why: They're thinking about how the book made them feel.

- I'm focused on them, but I remain quiet to give them a chance to ask questions. Why: I want to have a conversation with them.

Your Book Pitch

- Plan your response to the question, "What is this book about?"

- A two-minute pitch with a hook works well as a conversation starter for a single book or a series. I use a book pitch when I am a featured author at a book store.

Frequently Asked Questions with Suggested Answers

- Did you write all of these?

  - I sure did. Every single one. Which cover do you like the best?

  - Note: if they reply "good for you," or "I'll be back later," they want to move on. Tell them thank you. It's okay; they aren't your readers.

- Which one is your favorite? [The answer I use depends on my assessment of them.]

- Answer 1: That's like asking me which one of my four children is my favorite. {We laugh}

- Answer 2: I wrote them, so I love them all. {We laugh}

- Follow up: I'm more interested in which one you'd like.

- Can you help me pick out a book?

  - Sure! What kind of story do you like?

- What age group are these books for?

  - They're adult books, but I have a growing group of readers who are as young as fourteen that love the books.

Tip: These questions are fairly common.

How to Handle Non-Buyers

Not everyone who visits your booth will buy a book or even intend to buy a book, and that's okay. They might pick up a business card before they leave your booth so they don't hurt your feelings. Be gracious and thank them for stopping by.

If they tell you they just got there and need to see what else is there and they'll be back... they rarely will, but they frequently pick up a business card. I always tell them I look forward to seeing them again. Sometimes I ask them what their name is, so I can say, "See you later, Patty."

I'm pretty good at spotting them when they run past my booth later because I recognize people and remember names. I ignore my wicked side and don't even whisper, "Bye, Patty!"

- The Talker

At almost every event, a Talker comes to my booth with a story. I've learned to recognize them as they approach. They aren't there to buy or ask questions. They are there to talk about a subject which might be 'I'll tell you my life story so you can write my book for me,' or a long story which is almost always a monologue: 'I'll bet you didn't know...'

Tip #1: If a potential reader is walking toward my table, I say, "Really interesting. Excuse me," and immediately turn to smile at the approaching reader. I don't re-engage with the Talker.

Tip #2: I let them talk for a brief period if no one is around. Then when they take a breath (or sometimes I have to interrupt), I say,

"Really interesting. Thanks for stopping by. Enjoy the event." I divert my attention to an activity: re-organizing my books or looking in a bin.

- Haggler

Haggler #1: 'I buy books for $5.00.' I smile and nod.

Haggler #2: 'What's your best price?' I don't know if they're a true haggler or a bargain hunter, so I say, "My best price is when you buy at least three books because you save ten dollars."

A true haggler walks away.

Tip: I've never had a true haggler buy a book yet, but I'm still hopeful.

- New and Pre-published Author

New or pre-published authors occasionally stop by with questions, and I'll tell them the resources I've used and answer their questions the best I can. They don't linger, so I don't have to say "Excuse me."

- Special case: Aspiring Young Author

If I'm busy, I'll spot them hanging back waiting to talk to me. As soon as I can, I'll take time to chat with an aspiring young author and ask them questions about the story they are writing and answer their questions. They frequently have a hovering parent or grandparent who always thanks me.

Most readers who approach the table while I'm talking to a young author will wait and listen because they recognize the importance of encouragement for a budding author. If they pick up a book, Hubs steps in and makes the sale.

Customer Management Skills 101

Be Approachable

- Standing puts you at eye level, but please sit if you're tired or eating. You can still smile and make eye contact.

- Scrolling or talking on your phone sends the message: "I'm busy. Don't bother me."

Body Language Sells Books

What you say without speaking matters. A confident, friendly posture invites people in.

- Keep your shoulders relaxed. (I have to tell

myself this all the time.)

- Smile naturally.

- Pay attention to your customer.

Final Thoughts on Interaction

You don't have to be an extrovert to succeed at events. I'm the proof of that!

But you do need to be engaged, positive, and present. People buy from people they like. Be someone they'll remember, and not just because of your books, but because of the warm experience you gave them.

Chapter 10: Tailor Your Booth for Events

No two events are the same. A relaxed literary fair at a public library is a different world from a high-energy comic con packed with cosplay, just like a breezy outdoor crafts festival attracts a different crowd than a book-specific expo with celebrities.

You don't need a completely different booth for each; just make a few smart adjustments to **tailor your presence** for the space and audience.

This section breaks it down so you can show up prepared and with confidence, no matter where you're selling.

CRAFT & ART FESTIVALS

Events are typically outdoor but occasionally are indoor.

- **Audience** Casual browsers, families,

shoppers looking for handmade or one-of-a-kind items.

- **Vibe** Relaxed, local, often outdoors.

- **Expectations** Affordable prices, impulse buys, warm customer service.

Booth Tips

- Use an **inviting, colorful display** to stand out among pottery, soaps, and jewelry. Hint: your books are inviting and colorful.

- Feature signs like **"Signed by the Author"** or **"Local Author"** to catch curiosity.

- Offer **bundles and discounts**; these customers often buy on impulse.

- *Outdoor* Be sure your tent is **weather-ready** and your display can **withstand wind**.

- **Display Focus** Approachable and Friendly.

- **Engagement Style** Warm and Casual.

- **Best Sellers** Lower priced books and

bundles.

Book Fairs, Conferences, and Expos

Events are typically Indoor.

- **Audience** Book lovers, genre fans, book club members, serious readers.

- **Vibe** Literary, focused, shopping-oriented.

- **Expectations** Professional display, thoughtful branding, author engagement.

Booth Tips

- Use **genre signage** so browsers know instantly what you write.

- Offer **book club discussion guides**, **author or character cards**, or **"Read-Alike"** comparison signs to help readers decide.

- Make sure your **newsletter QR code sign-up** is front and center.

- **Display Focus** Clean and genre-specific.

- **Engagement Style** Professional and direct.

- **Best Sellers** Series, bundles, signed editions.

Literary Conferences

Indoor Events.

- **Audience** Writers, educators, librarians, book professionals.

- **Vibe** Reflective, academic, networking-heavy.

- **Expectations** Professionalism, literary merit, deeper conversations.

Booth Tips

- Focus less on flashy displays and more on **clean, polished materials**.

- Bring **media kits, sell sheets** (online graphic design tools have templates), or **library order forms** if applicable.

- Be prepared to **talk about process**, **craft**, or **publishing**, not just plot.

- Even if sales are slow, focus on **building relationships** and **making connections**.

- **Display Focus** Polished and minimalist.

- **Engagement Style** Thoughtful and nuanced.

- **Best Sellers** Literary fiction, memoir, process guides.

COMIC BOOK, GAMING, AND GENRE CONVENTIONS

Indoor Events.

- **Audience**:Pop culture fans, cosplayers, collectors, avid genre readers.

- **Vibe** Energetic, eclectic, crowded, costume-heavy.

- **Expectations** Genre enthusiasm, visual appeal, personality.

Booth Tips

- Lean into your **genre branding**. Dark for horror, neon for sci-fi, lush for fantasy, etc.

- Bring **vertical banners** with character art, catchy taglines, or cover montages.

- Offer **genre-specific swag**. Buttons, postcards, trading cards, signed art prints.

- Prepare a **fast, fun pitch** that hooks attention quickly in a crowded hall.

- Wear a **themed outfit or subtle cosplay** that fits the convention, and if it fits your brand.

- *Bonus Tip:* Comic cons are a great place to sell **first-in-series**, **novellas**, **RPG**, or even **'zines**. Keep your prices conference-friendly and your booth eye-catching.

- **Display Focus** Bold and graphic.

- **Engagement Style** Fast, fun, fandom aware.

- **Best Sellers** Fiction, novellas, video and

tabletop games, merchandise.

Library & School Events

Indoor Events.

- **Audience** Families, educators, students, librarians.

- **Vibe** Quiet, friendly, community-focused.

- **Expectations** Approachable pricing, clear age categories, thoughtful interaction.

Booth Tips

- Label books by **age group** (Adult, YA, MG, etc.).

- Be ready to answer: "Is this appropriate for a 13-year-old?"

- Offer **school or library discounts** if possible.

- Keep **themes and content clearly explained** on signs to build trust with educators and parents.

- **Display Focus** Clear and approachable.

- **Engagement Style** Respectful and informative.

- **Best Sellers** Age-appropriate books, nonfiction.

OTHER TYPES OF EVENT BOOTHS

- Half table

Indoor Events.

With a half table, you are sharing your table with another author. If the event shares the contact information for your table companion, contact the other author before the event. Each author is responsible for selling their books.

- Multi-author booth

Outdoor or Indoor Events.

A multi-author booth is a co-op style of selling books of multiple genres typically sponsored by a local author group.

Authors are frequently limited to one or two titles and only a few books of each title at the booth.

Authors rotate staffing the booth to avoid stuffing the booth with authors!

The style of table setup frequently is U-shaped with the opening with the U facing the front of the booth so that readers can go into the booth and browse the tables. Sales are recorded and paid to the authors after the event ends.

Tip: Let 'Have Books Will Travel' be your motto

You don't need a whole new booth for every type of event. Instead, think like a traveler. Same suitcase, just a different outfit for the occasion.

With a flexible setup, well-crafted signage, and genre-appropriate engagement, you'll be ready to sell books and make a lasting impression anywhere readers gather.

Chapter 11: Final Thoughts & Next Steps

Hopefully, you're feeling more prepared and more excited about selling your books in person.

Whether you're still planning your first event or you've already done a few, this final chapter is here to remind you that you don't have to be perfect. You just have to show up and smile.

What I Wish I'd Known When I Started

Looking back, there are a few things I wish someone had told me before my first event. Here they are, so you can start one step ahead.

1. Planning is good, but not everything goes as planned. Every event builds your confidence, your reputation, and your reach. Keep going.

2. People will remember you, even the non-buyers. Someone may walk past your booth ten times before stopping. Someone may take your card and buy a book online six months later. They may come looking for you the following year. You're building visibility, not just sales.

3. Every event is unique; even the same event a year later. Adjust as you go.

4. Not everyone is your reader, and not everyone reads. *That is so shocking to me.* You're not out there for everyone. You're there for your readers.

5. There are good sales days and bad sales days. There are more good than bad.

WHEN SOMETHING GOES WRONG

Because it will. Eventually, you'll forget something, the wind will try to blow away your tent, the noise level indoors is unbearable, or sales will be slower than expected.

Here's how to handle it:

- Stay calm. You'll be surprised how many problems can be solved with duct tape, zip ties, or a borrowed chair. Also, nearby shopping is your friend. (Hello Walmart, Lowes, and Home Depot) We've had to augment our weights for high wind with concrete blocks and buy a cash box because we forgot ours.

- Focus on what you can control: your attitude, your customer service, your response to challenges.

- Laugh it off when you can. Every vendor has a story about a "disaster day." You're earning yours.

- Low sales? Maybe the event had a scheduling conflict with a more popular event, or your spot was in the worst possible location (being across from a row of stinky porta potties kills sales. I can show you the numbers.); the weather was too hot, too cold, or too rainy, or it just wasn't the right event for you. Whatever it was, it's feedback, not failure.

Keep Going

Every author who has found success selling books in person started with one table, one book, and second thoughts.

- Your readers are out there. You just haven't met them all yet.

- Every event is a chance to connect. Even if sales are light, your presence matters.

- You're building something. One sale at a time, one reader at a time, one story at a time.

Next Steps

Build Your Data

Create records of each event
- Packing checklist customized for your setup.

- Price and inventory sheet for each event.

- Photo log of your booth displays.

- Event feedback form of sales, audience, weather, rebooking notes.

Prepare for your next event

- Create a vendor binder with maps, schedules, and contacts for upcoming events.

- Invest in a banner.

- Join local vendor or indie author groups online.

Final Tip: The more you lean into your author business, the more confident you'll feel about selling books and being an author. Guaranteed.

Chapter 12: Sample Schedule

A smooth event starts with good planning. This sample schedule checklist walks you through what to do and when, starting with over two months before the event and ending with the most important step: celebrate!

Whether you're new to festivals or just want a clear timeline to follow, this guide can help you stay sane, stay organized, and maybe you'll even enjoy venturing out into the wild where the readers are!

2+ Months Before Event

- Apply for Event.

8 Weeks

- Inventory books on hand.

- Determine the number of books for 2 events.

- Order books.

<u>6 Weeks</u>

- Determine the price to sell books; adjust retailers as necessary.

- Determine the payment methods you will accept.

- Buy a locking cash box.

- Determine the amount and denominations of bills to have in your cashbox for change.

- Install an app on your phone to accept credit cards.

- Test the app with your smart phone with a $1.00 sale from yourself. Note you will only be able to accept tap to pay cards. Some of the older debit cards require a card reader.

- If outdoor event, borrow tent; if you plan on mostly outdoor events, buy a lower cost tent.

- Borrow or buy a table unless you already have one.

- Borrow or buy folding or camping chair(s) unless you already have them.

<u>5 Weeks</u>

- Set up tent, if you're going to an outdoor event.

- Place the table and chair(s) under the tent. Clean table if not new.

- Take down tent and put it back into its cover.

- Create and order business cards. Order only 200. (You may change your business card after an event or two.)

<u>4 Weeks</u>

- Determine how you will display your signs.

- Create price and author signs.

- Gather the change for your cashbox and fill it.

- Create a list of items to load for the event.

<u>3 Weeks</u>

- Check ordered books as they arrive. Return damaged books.

- Determine your safe weight for a bin with books.

- Determine the number of bins you will need.

- Buy or use bins you have. Don't exceed your maximum weight of books per bin.

2 Weeks

- Set up your tent *outdoor event*. (I know this is a repeat)

- Set up your table with a tablecloth and put your signs on the table. Admire your work.

- Fold up your table and tablecloth.

- Take down your tent and put it in its cover.

- Using your loading list, load everything into your vehicle including empty bins.

- Unload your vehicle unless there are items you don't mind hauling around for two weeks.

- Put books into bins. Add table items to bins. (Tablecloth, signs, notebook and pen to record sales, business cards, etc.)

- Revise your loading list if needed.

- If you're feeling nervous about your credit card app, practice another $1.00 sale.

1 Week
- Plan your lunch and snacks.

2 Days
- Load your vehicle with everything except books.

Day Before Event
- Load bins with books.

Event Day
- Pack and load lunch, snacks, and water.

- Load cashbox.

- Double-check your packing list.

At the Event
- Unload.

- Set Up.

- Check cell coverage.

- Take a photo after you're set up.

- HAVE FUN.

<u>Event Day: When You Arrive at Home</u>
- Unload books.

- Unload cashbox.

<u>Day After the Event</u>
- Unload everything else.

- Record your impressions of the event.

- Count the money in the cashbox and return it to your starting amount.

- Determine if you need to reorder any books.

Celebrate!

That's it!

Every event is a little different, and over time, you'll tweak this schedule to fit your own pace and style. But having a checklist gives you a solid starting point and peace of mind that you're not forgetting something important, like, say, your cashbox (we've done that so you don't have to.).

The more events you attend, the more you will learn, and the easier it will be for you to adjust on the fly!

Until then, keep this list handy, give yourself some grace because you deserve it, and don't forget to enjoy the ride. You're building something wonderful, one event at a time.

Thank You for Reading

Thank you for spending time with *Have Books Will Travel*. I hope this guide has given you the confidence, tools, and ideas to make your next in-person event successful and most importantly, fun.

Everything I've shared is from my personal experiences. Just because something works for me doesn't make it a magic pill that will work for everyone, so take advantage of my wins and scars and use what works for you.

If you have questions, suggestions, or stories of your own in-person selling experiences, I'd love to hear from you. Every event is a little different, and your feedback not only helps me improve future editions, but might also inspire new tips for fellow authors.

If you found this book helpful, I'd be truly grateful if you'd leave a quick review. You know how important they are, and reviews will help other authors discover this guide.

You can reach me through my website at judithabarrett dot com or give me a shout on Facebook. I'm there because my readers are there.

Have you heard the old saying, 'Break a leg'?

From one author-vendor to another, rip a page!

Judith

Acknowledgments

This guide is dedication to Labor because without his support, this guide would be nonexistent.

A big ole rip of the page to Ben Wolf because without his brilliant examples and encouragement, I would never have gone ALL IN on selling direct.

More About the Author

Judith A. Barrett, an award-winning storyteller, crafts gripping series that weave her thriller, mystery, romantic, cozy mystery, historic fiction, and post-apocalyptic science fiction novels with unexpected twists and unforgettable characters.

Her passions are writing and connecting with readers at lively weekend arts and crafts festivals, sharing stories as bold and eclectic as she is.

Sequestered on a quiet Georgia farm with her amazingly supportive husband, two loyal dogs (very good boys), and a flock of spirited chickens, Judith watches the sunset from her writing spot while the stories surge through her fingers and onto the keyboard.

You know, just another writer who doesn't follow the rules.

Her motto: *You keep reading; I'll keep writing!*

Barrett Book Shop

BarrettBookShop.com

An Author-owned Book Shop with Exclusive
Bargains and Deals

Judith A. Barrett Books
You keep reading; I'll keep writing
Maggie Sloan Thriller Series
Grid Down Survival Series
Jenna Ross Thriller Series
Riley Malloy Mystery Series
Wren and Rascal Mystery Series
Donut Lady Cozy Mystery Series
Speakeasy Secrets, A Jazz Age Mystery